Aduke, the 'Nothing' Girl

Victoria Eniola

Kayin Publishing

Aduke, the Nothing Girl

This is a work of fiction. Names, characters, places, and incidents either are the product of the author's imagination or are used fictitiously. Any resemblance to actual persons, living or dead, events, or locales is entirely coincidental.

Illustrated by Efe Peters

First edition June 2020

Dear Readers,

You are holding in your hands, a special piece of my heart – I thought about you while writing this. YOU, who believe you have no right to feel the way you do. YOU, who may be frustrated with your emotions, YOU who feel the sting of the unkind words that have been said to you.

Here is your friendly reminder to use your voice without shame because we all need to hear what is on your heart.

I hope you are taking excellent care of your body, heart & mind – because you are so worthy

My hope is that this book starts meaningful conversations & in the meantime, I will be putting in the work to be my best self.

All my love & sunshine,

V

DEDICATION:

Dela,

You are a dream come true & Auntie bestie absolutely adores you!

Special thanks to the cheerleaders in my life - Family and friends. For encouraging me to fill up the spaces I once apologised for. For listening to my heart and showing up with grace.

I love you all,

H.R.H

x

"There is no greater agony than bearing an untold story inside you..."

—Maya Angelou

"Aduke, you're failing maths," Ms Ngozi said.

Aduke didn't say anything. She just looked down at the teacher's brown table with its many scratches. She didn't want to look up at Ms Ngozi's face because she didn't want to see her teacher giving her the pity look. Everyone knew Ms Ngozi's pity face; it would make you feel terrible for failing. Aduke didn't want that.

"Look at me, Aduke. What is the problem?" Ms Ngozi asked.

"Nothing," Aduke said.

"It can't be nothing, Aduke. You have been saying 'nothing' for four weeks now. Yet, your work is not getting better. You're better than this, and we both know it," Ms Ngozi said.

This time, Aduke kept her mouth shut. She knew if she opened her mouth, she would cry and that would not be fine.

"Talk to me, Aduke. Let's see how I can help you." Ms Ngozi was a very persistent teacher and would not stop asking until you gave her an answer. However, Aduke did not intend to give in. She didn't want anyone feeling bad. She was sure she could handle her problems herself, so Aduke just stared down at the table and scratched the surface with her nails while ignoring Ms Ngozi.

After a really long time trying to get an answer out of Aduke, Ms Ngozi gave up and told her she could go.

"Thank you, ma," Aduke said, and she walked out of the classroom, careful not to look at the kind teacher's face.

As she left, Ms Ngozi called out to her with one last message: "Exams start next week. At this rate, you won't pass. You must sit up, or you may have to repeat the class. Don't forget, you can talk to me anytime."

When the teacher was done talking, Aduke nodded and hurried on outside.

She was thin, even though she ate a lot of food. Her mother was always stuffing her with food and hoping she would add some weight, but Aduke stayed skinny. When she walked, it looked as though her clothes were hanging onto her, and not like she was wearing them.

She walked past the playground, past the car park where so many other students were meeting up with their parents, and she thought about the things Ms Ngozi had said. Like she was actually going to tell Ms Ngozi what was going on at home. What good would it do? She just needed to work harder at maths and that was all her teacher needed to know.

For a 12-year-old, Aduke was pretty serious about many things. She knew the problem at home had not gone away. She also decided she was going to find a way to study more.

As she got to the entrance to her home, Aduke Bello took a deep breath, pushed the gate open and went inside.

The grass had not been cut in days, and Aduke decided to pull out as much of it as she could with her hands later that day. She could hear the yelling even before she got to the front door, so she went around the back and went in through the kitchen door.

Aduke's father had just lost his job, and he was very cranky all the time. Aduke's mother had just had a baby, Aduke's little brother, and she was not in much better spirits than her husband.

Every day, they yelled at each other and forgot all about Aduke. Aduke was a good child, and she could make her own meals and clean the house, but no one was paying any attention to her. No one asked about her day at school or looked at her homework. Studying was so hard to do with all the yelling, but Aduke was not about to tell anyone about that. Only babies cry when something happens to them. That was what she was told. Aduke was fine, and she could take care of herself.

She went into the living room and picked up her baby brother from his cradle. He was so soft and cute, and Aduke wanted to hold him forever.

"Oh, hi Aduke. You're back. Hope you remembered what I told you to buy?"

"Ah, Aduke. Come and help me bring my phone charger" her father said from the couch.

Before she could respond to any of them, they were yelling at each other again.

Aduke was very tired. She really wished someone would help her with schoolwork or fix her hair. Still, she wasn't going to say anything. Only little babies cry for attention.

The next day, at school, Aduke got her science homework back and saw that she had failed. She felt so bad, she wanted to cry. So, she ran out of the class and into the hallway. There, she bumped into Ms Ngozi. The kind teacher took one look at her and took her to her office. As soon as she sat in the chair, Aduke began to cry.

She told Ms Ngozi about home and all the trouble. She said to her that she didn't want to cause anyone any more trouble than they already had. Ms Ngozi quickly called Aduke's parents to come over to the school.

Before they got there, Ms Ngozi said these words that Aduke would never forget: "It's okay to say how you feel, as long as the way you say it does not hurt anyone. When you keep these things inside you, it's like filling a jug with water and not pouring it out. Soon, the water will spill and make a big mess. The mess, in this case, could be your grades."

When her parents came, they were very sorry. They had been dealing with so much that they forgot how much their daughter needed them, and because she never said anything, they did not know she needed help. They promised to do better, and Aduke promised to share how she was feeling, rather than just say "nothing."

After letting people into her world and letting them know her struggles, Aduke felt like a huge weight had been lifted from her shoulders. She found she was able to concentrate easier, and her grades lifted almost immediately. Although the problems at home were still there, her parents made a conscious effort to help their daughter and made sure their difficulties didn't affect their Aduke.

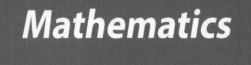

ABOUT AUTHOR

Victoria Eniola is a Nigerian writer who is very excited about her first published book. She is determined to create safe spaces for children to thrive through her love for music and storytelling.

She is a proud mama to her goldfish, Princess Greta & her love for Whitney Houston runs deep.

Victoria's life journey has taken her all over the world but home to her is Nigeria. In her free time, Victoria is most likely watching a Yoruba movie or laughing at the memes her friends send her. She has been writing poetry for many years and although hasn't been the best steward of her words, is now ready to do better.

Victoria hopes you enjoy this book & is so grateful you exist x

Printed in Poland
by Amazon Fulfillment
Poland Sp. z o.o., Wrocław

60356080R00019